MOMENTS

WORKS BY
MICHAEL BRANT DEMARIA

PROSE
EVER FLOWING ON
HORNS AND HALOS
PEACE WITHIN

MUSIC CD'S
THE RIVER
OCEAN
GAIA
SIYOTANKA
BINDU
THE MAIDEN OF STONEHENGE
IN THE FLOW
SOLACE
HEART OF SILENCE

PLAYS
THE BREEZE
SIYOTANKA
THE MAIDEN OF STONEHENGE

POETRY
MOMENTS

MOMENTS

Poems By

MICHAEL BRANT DEMARIA

ONTOS WORLD PRESS

ISBN: 978-0-9802196-0-9 First Edition
Library of Congress Control Number First Edition: 2008920100

ISBN: 978-0-9802196-2-3 2nd Edition 2016
Library of Congress Control Number 2nd Edition: 2016910412

ISBN: 978-0-9802196-3-0 2nd Edition/Ebook 2016

Poetry/Spirituality/Philosophy

Printed in the United States of America

First Printing 2008
Second Printing 2014
2nd Edition and e-book 2016

First Published in 2008
Ontos World Press
512 E. Zaragoza St.
Pensacola, FL 32502
USA

Dedicated to all who dwell or seek
to dwell in the pure possibility and divinity of
this moment...

CONTENTS

I. BEING MOMENTS

II. TWILIGHT MOMENTS

CONTENTS

III. JOURNEY MOMENTS

IV. EARTH MOMENTS

V. Human Moments

"We have only this moment,
sparkling like a star in our hand,
and melting like a snowflake."

~ Marie Beyon Ray

BEING MOMENTS

SINGING YOUR NAME

Sunlight shimmers
through the leaves...
melting everything
around me...

There is no fear...
in this melting
just rapt attention...
and awe at the miracle
of seeing...

Moments,
come, one after another,
as if a dam has given way,
upstream....

It's too much, sometimes...
this beholding,
the miracle of being
washing though me...

Images, sounds
and wordless whispers...
all here...
in this moment...

all...singing Your name...

Ocean of Bliss

Opening the
soft petals of
this moment...

beholding
melts
me,

breathing...
unfolds...
me....

dissolving solidity...
liquifying me...

Presence
flowers,
blossoming
into fullness...

flowing in waves,
radiating outward...

Ocean of bliss...

Can You Remember

Can you remember?
...it was not so long ago...
when space stretched out all around you
cradling the softness of you...
and all that your body loved
was around you...whispering...

"Welcome...Welcome..."

Can you remember?
...it was not so long ago...
when the sun drenched you
with kisses...
and the wind cradled you in its arms...
whispering...

"Ahhhh..."

And, can you remember?
...it was not that long ago...
when you knew who you really were...
the silent spaces between words and things...

Yes...and then, in that vastness,

you remember...

EVERY TIME I DIE

Somehow,

every time I die,
I become more myself...

Somehow,

every time I die,
I become more
in line
with God...

LOVE'S BLESSING

The mind struggles
with the eternal
rising and falling of
who we are,
where we are,
how we are,
questioning *everything* ...

Can there ever be
certainty,
in all of this revolving
eternity?

The heart answers,

"Who needs
certainty, when the
wind caresses my
hair with the delicate
tender waves of
love that course through
the air...

Love needs no
explanation,
no final destination...

it is...
and for that,
we are...
blessed."

AMNESS

Breathing,
I remember,
beyond memory...
riding
ancient river
of breath....

Space dissolves,
time expands...
eyes soften...

Speechless presence....
radiating...in all directions...

I am...
becomes amness...
and...

bliss...

THIS LOVE

In and amongst *this* Love
there are no shoulds, oughts and musts...
no fears that rattle the mind...
no judgments to poison the soul...

In and amongst *this* Love
the kindness of Creation
reaches its tender hands
in welcome...

In and amongst *this* Love
I am cradled in the vastness

In and amongst *this* Love
all-that-is sings my nameless name...

In and amongst *this* Love
I lie down
worn out and tired,
to be refreshed by gentleness,
and rapture

In and amongst *this* Love
I finally cease to think,
or speak...

In and amongst *this* Love...

Melting Fear

Throughout history
separateness
has plagued us...

Like some massive
unfurling of hate...

This against that,
him against her,
me against you,
struggle and strife,
bloodying and bruising us...

The cry comes loud,
and sometimes in whimpers,
"how do I know which way to go,
how do I know whom to trust!"...

And the battle ensues...
until we sense fear around
every corner there is something
uncertain, treacherous and dangerous...

Then...
like some luminescent being,
unfolding before us...
radiating out in all directions...
we find ourselves in the presence
of a oneness so deep...
so vast...
we melt...

and the fear that has
haunted us...
begins to recede...

Until there is nothing left
but the faint whispers
of a forgotten nightmare...
like the last thin lines of
smoke
from a fire that has
burned through
the night...

and even those ashes
somehow
cool now,
join the dance...
and sing a new day into
existence...

A day where love
melts all fear...

INEXHAUSTIBLE

There is something...
something inexhaustible
at the root, at the core
of this moment.

Inexhaustible,
like the infinite sea
existing
before me...
before I came to be

Inexhaustible
as the infinite sky...
stretching out before me
continuing
beyond where I can see...

But, this me,
this I...
this am
that I am
spirals around
this core,
this root,
I speak of...

That I recede
back into
this *inexhaustible* something
perhaps no-thing...
no violent death

but, no matter what,
it is...*inexhaustible*.

This something
that is a no-thing...
lets me taste
the infinite...
immortal...
peace within me ...

Its core rings out,
deeply, loudly,
silently...

reaching me
where no other
can...

Encompassing
vast endless
expanses
of stars...
and infinite space...

In this inexhaustible
something
from which everything
grows...

Here...
I am peace.

No wound
no wrenching
of my soul
or any other's
wavers me,
or shatters
me...

This inexhaustible
no-thingness sustains
and nourishes.

For in it
I see all places
all times...
all things...
and no-thing...

BROKEN BREAD

There is a wisdom in things
like the stillness of a lake,
or mist rising from the sea...

A vastness,
lying in wait
for those moments
the veil of tears fall...

and we see things,
in a moment
as they really are...

but, ah, so brief,
like lightning,
in the distance,
is this great presence of God
waiting to be known.

So much
we can neither grasp,
nor hold...

yet,
somehow,
this smallness that we are,
is necessary
so we can be broken,
and thus known,

by that which is beyond us,

and yes, inside of us,
dying, yes dying, to be known.

Break me open this daymake
Lord,

me bread for your
table,

and allow me to remember,
your presence,
flickering in the distance,
which is really,

inside
of me...

SEASON OF THE SOUL

The sky's clear
I can see again...
The darkness gave
birth to the light...
The silence to the song...

Impenetrable by reason...
the heart beats on...
Knowing something unknowable,
speaking a language forgotten
dancing a dance half
seen...

On the other side lies
the missing pieces...
we travel there half knowing
just hoping...hoping for a
glimpse of where the beating began...

and where in its incessant
rhythmic calling it is
taking us.

Do we dare follow?
Entranced by a dancing
goddess hidden in the shadows...
asking us to surrender all we've known,
all we've heard tell of what is real.

Can we, can we,
breathe, move,
sing and dance out
the rhythms of eternity?

Do we have faith?
faith in the night,
faith in rhythm,
faith in love...
faith in life...

The life of the soul...
transcending death
seeing it for what it is...
simply...
clearly...

a season of the soul...

Dying To Be Born

There is a time afoot,
where the ancient wisdom
echoes the knowing
quaking in your bones,

dying to be...

There is a time afoot...
for opening the
treasure locked within,

The new world
will not be made
of brick and mortar,

It is the place
found by
turning within...

Glancing
around the corner
of your own eyes...

Listen closely
to the spaces
between your thoughts,

There...
you will hear the hum,
the stirring
of God...

Dying to be born,
in yes... your flesh...

Now

I wonder if
this collection
of moments
called life,

fragile,
ephemeral, and
impermanent,

hides something,
eternal...endless...
inexplicable...

Like some wild,
exotic, vast and
unimaginable
spaciousness...

This is what
enshrouds
every moment...

And, do we,
don't we perpetually
miss the caress
this moment provides?

Ignoring
the Mystery
this moment
cradles us in...

Who we are,
and can be...
and perhaps,
have always been...

Stop,
breathe...
Love this moment...
and no other...

and enter
the kingdom...
now...

True Silence

Out of the woods of remembrance
where the path of wonder is found
you will hear for the first time
true silence.

A pinpoint of stillness
merging the forest wind
with the sound
of your own breathing.

In this silence,
the voices of the ancient ones
share the secret of Life.

And the shadows
of your own language
are no longer spoken by the child.

Hearing so differently now
the silence
nature sings
reminding you
of Being...

TWILIGHT MOMENTS

BREATHING MIDNIGHT

Around midnight,
I breathe silently,
slowly,

Noticing
in between
the in breath
and the out...

A moment,
suspended in time,
where I no longer am...

Then,
like some river
vast, swift moving,
I am carried by
something
other than me...

In the next breath,
the endlessness
ends...and life continues
toward some
unknown destination...

And, yet...
I am changed...
by this place
at midnight,
this space,
between moments...
where I am,
amness...

nothingness...
and...
everything...

impossible,
and true...

Dream Droplets

Breathing...
being...
unfolding...

Like dew
appearing
before
the morning light...

I find wholeness...
in the early morning
darkness...
as I awake...

Dream
droplets
emerging
all over my body...

Ripe for the
licking and
lapping up
of my soul...

This morning,
God is near...
and I am clear
on who...
I am...

NIGHT REMEMBERING

I seek so often...
that I come around
again to this place
half forgetting,
half remembering,
who I have been...
why I am here...

Then the mist descends
again, and I too am
but a creature of
the night, trying my
best to survive in
the blackness,
foraging for
a little food,
and a den
of soft down
to call my own...

To belong finally,
to this night and
mist that enfolds
all of my most
preciously held plans
and seemingly endless
doings...

In this night
my soul begins
to remember,
where it is I am from...
and, moreover,
where all
these lives are
gradually taking
me...
again...
and again...

It is then,
light and shadow,
day and night,
joy and sorrow...
play together a
song sweeter,
more whole,
than anything
sung before...

Night Rapids

Lonely nights...
dark abyss...
sometimes I curse you and
this life...

Then like some strange and wondrous
visitation in the night...between
the cries, the shouts, and tears...
there is a sound, so silent, so sweet,
that I realize the "something more than me"
quietly moving through the rapids of this night...

It is then I reach out my hand
into the dark...
and call your name...
and there, abiding presence
you touch me...

though...
without hands...
without body...
and it is then...
that I realize...

The place I have been absent from,
all the time I have been here...
in this place...
this space...
called life...

Deliver me...home
dear presence of the night...
safely upon the shores of that which
I have always been, but have so easily
denied...

WAKING

There are a thousand ways
to wake to this world...
from the other...

Sometimes it is effortless,
like morning mist rising from the sea,
or the sun evaporating
shadows from the night before...

Of course,
more often than not,
it is hard, grueling and difficult work,
like a jackhammer on concrete...

Sometimes,
like a heavy burden,
because there is so much of me,
that longs to stay in the other,
more weightless world...

To all of a sudden remember,
yes, I, for now, am still a body...
with aches and pains, and struggle -
blood and bone,
muscle and sinew...
and of course...hunger...

Sometimes,
It's somewhere between effort
and effortless...

It is as if...
I could stay suspended between

the worlds forever.
As if, somehow that is where
I am most at home...in the twilight...

And...sometimes,
like this morning,
like those moments,
when you're just waiting,
somewhere on a long and dusty
road, where no one seems to travel,
feeling lost and alone,
a presence arrives.
The one you have waited for
all your life...

And you can't say no...
and yet, you know it won't be easy...
and you go...
not so much up...
as forward and...
down...
spiraling...
towards the earth.

Waking up this way,
Is like a tree growing down,
into some dark longing,
a place unfamiliar,
though I call it home...

Today...
is such a day.

CIRCLING THE DAWN

The nights grow
until I can barely make out
what I once knew...

Circling the dawn,
the awakening begins.
One dream fades...
another unfolds...

I too grow
in this darkness
that seems too long...

But, then again,
incubation sows seeds
that only patience
can unfold...

I reach out to trust
this unknowing, this
bittersweet surrender...

There are no promises here,
of painless nights
and restful sleep...

Only the promise of
a heart beating a rhythm
that knows no rest...

I've always known
the soul never sleeps...
and nourishes itself in
those places I have ignored...

So tonight,
while the dawn
plays hide and seek,
remaining but a promise
of that other dream,
my waking life,
I will find solace in
this longer night,
and whisper to the presence
that brings all of this
to be...

Listening,
listening...
for the echo...
in the silence,
of this night...

Flashes

Between
the darkness and the light,
life proceeds in flashes,
like some strange dance
between the worlds.

A terrible wakefulness
that knows the limits
of this life which crashes
against the shore of our unwavering need for
significance...

These are the times
to breathe, and
feel the very depth of
Being coursing through our veins...

To know we matter,
even in our defeat...

Waking is a strange sleep,
when the awareness
of the many worlds in One
parade across the mind....

ONENESS

The silent places
of oneness
catch me unaware...
like a breeze on a still day...
like raindrops,
without a cloud in the sky...

Like an oasis
in the desert,
or that barely visible
edge of light in the dark...

Then...
when I least expect it...
I'm speechless...
because once again...
I've disappeared...
disappeared...
into You...

FORGOTTEN LANGUAGE

Sunrise...
Sunset...

The scent of spring rain...
in a lush pine forest...

The sound of stillness...
in the first light of morning...

Thoughts...images...presence...
half asleep...half awake...
between the worlds...
life speaks...

A language all but
forgotten...

Nature's hieroglyphs,
singing over and over...
"I love you...I love you..."

A love so great,
it draws the sun out of the sea..
across the sky,
and into the world...

Again...and again...

Sunrise...
Sunset...

Too Many Words

There is already
too much talking,
too many words pointing
to places and things
that distract us
inevitably from the place
from which they emerge...

I suppose that's true...

So...here's to you...
sweet silence...

SUBTLE TRANCE

I recline, give up
and tell death,
"You win."

Sinking, I quietly fall...
until the whispering
solitude reverberates through
every cell, beating some ancient
rhythm, dancing some far off
forgotten swaying...

Love is a subtle trance here...
pulsating through the rock,
speaking through the silence...
The crevices hide forgotten parts of my
soul, I try desperately to retrieve...

Something is calling me...
someone is stalking me...

I turn...

Nothingness....

Moments

Moments...
like mist...
cleanse my tired
worn body...

Finding within
places unheard and
untouched...

How is such bliss
possible...
when the sound
of silence becomes
a symphony...
echoing eternity...

I am speechless...
at such beauty...

Could Heaven be
made of such mist?

EARLY MORNING STILLNESS

The familiar yawn
of early morning stillness...

The water moves
slowly...
as the tide
comes in,
imperceptibly.
Yet, like this morning
grows...

The wind makes
love to the branches
ever so lightly...
coaxing them,

and preparing
them for the
first rays of light...

My eyes adjust,
opening
and wondering
how a moment ago
I was on a rocky cliff
in Hawaii...
surf lapping at my feet.

And now,
the silence spaces
give way
to a place
only I can inhabit
only I can breathe into,
only I know the
secret of...

And the day waits
for me,
to grow into her...

Like the water
and the breeze
called by
subtle movements
from beyond...

JOURNEY MOMENTS

All I Ask

Lord,
I promise
to do
my best
to stop
hiding from you...

I have lived
my life in
circular
currents,
avoiding
the path
that leads
directly to you...

The river,
has called,
and I have
refused
to answer...

I have settled,
for riding
these endless
eddies,
and whirlpools...
that take me around...
and around...
and around you...

I hear,
now,
what you want
from me...
what you require
of me...

and it's not easy...
in fact,
it rocks
my whole world...

and I sit
half terrified,
half ecstatic...
at what
I hear
you dimly
whisper...

No,
they are no longer
whispers...
they are
shouts of
divine
awakening...

yes...
yes...
yes...

I will...
I will go down...
the river...

I only ask
you stay
by my side...
all the way...
until
I am ready

to pour this
fragile
body
into your
endless
keeping...

I love you...
more than all
I've ever known...

Like a hidden
love affair
that grows in
the silent
places,
where the
light of
reason can
not destroy
the fragile
roots
of
truth...

This night,
the roots of myself sink
deeply into you...

Persistent Stranger

Funny how the soul knocks...
like a persistent stranger
at the door...
dying to be known...
starving for attention...
hungry to be found...

Far away from the distractions
that silence those rhythmic
rappings at the back door of our life...

Oh, how seldom prepared we are
when we find our way to that door...
and let go of the fear of finding
what has been knocking...
all this time...
waiting...

The door opens...
the gasp comes...
as we breathe in
the presence of the great
discovery...

Weak kneed and alone
we stand...

and the soul finally makes its presence
known...
and the knocking becomes
a radiance...

awesome in its completeness
and there is no place to go,
nothing to hide...
and we stand naked...
aware...
awake...
alone...
certain we will die
from this encounter...
that remains bigger
than us...

The weeping begins...
and there is
no longer knocking,
but the cascading sound
of a thousand waterfalls
taking us home...

FOOTBRIDGE

Do you remember
the look of your boots
in the dust?

The trail was long,
it was hot
and dry...

You came across a
footbridge
and on the bridge
you felt words
inside
trapped and begging
to be freed...

"These steps,
these...steps...
are the first steps
of my...
new life..."

and as you said them,
a smile emerged,
as you strode your
way through the dust...

and somehow, you knew
when you reached
the other side
nothing would ever be
the same
again...

BEARING FRUIT

After you begin to speak
about the truths
deep within...

The outside ever so slowly,
like a seedling growing
into a sapling,
begins to resemble the inside...

The call to bear fruit
becomes more urgent
as the outline of the tree
you are to be takes shape
and form...

and it becomes simply
what you must do...

To be who you are,
and bear the fruit,
you came to bear...

Original Voice

Each moment is a note
in the song of today...
rising and playing...

The many voices
of me...
intermingling with
Being...

The hum of God
is the canvas,
and the sounds come
full formed.

My original voice,
crazy enough
to reach all the
way to the other
side of things,

as if echoing,
the place from
which it came...

If You Are A Lover

If you are a lover in this world,
a true lover,
who cannot help but see
the incarnation of God
in the face of everyone you meet...

You will have your heart
scattered upon the winds of time,
destroyed a thousand ways,
until the fleshy core of your being
is made raw and exposed for all to see...

If you are a lover in this world...
life will change you...
and you will either resent the process of
opening...
or learn to give yourself over to it...

After years of struggle
the face of the beloved will
grow ever so slowly into
your own eyes...
shining out at the world...

being found...
every moment,
of every day...

Lost Voices

Here I sit...
fate's handiwork
all around...

Tell-tale signs of
what has been missed...
lost...

Those voices in
me that no
longer speak...

Hiding like
some scared,
wild animal
in the bush...

Invisible,
out of sight...
silent...

Yet,
there remains
a faint scent,
of some other
presence here,

knocking at the back
door...

But, I say to myself,
"There is nobody out

there"...nobody comes to
the back door anymore...

The scent turns into
a scratch
as my heart
beats a little louder...

And I know
all too well...
there is a lone presence
intent on getting in...

Can my love
overcome
the terror
that paralyzes
me in my warm bed,
freeing me to
descend
into the cold dark
house of myself?

To finally,
completely
open the back door
to the night air,
and the wild creatures,
living in my own
backyard...

Or will I rather lie
here, not sleeping,
not waking,
caught in
the moment
before creation...

Two Medicine

That day
is etched in my soul...
seared into my heart.

I had been lost,
half asleep,
not knowing
anything...

And then,
on that lonely road,
in the middle of nowhere,
I made my way
to a lake called
Two Medicine,

Two Medicine,
where I had come,
empty, broken, and alone...

So much effort,
so much struggle
to break free...
so many chains
that had imprisoned me...

To take that step,
that first step,
that real step,
my...step...

Now,
years later,
I see once again,
those boots,
in the dust,
walking toward
Two Medicine...

CLIMBING A RIVER

As Dante says,
when scaling a cliff
becomes as easy
as floating down a river,
you will have arrived
where this
journey
was meant to take you...

The soft
overcomes
the hard...

Like the endless
streams and rivers
flowing and etching
their way
through the mountain.

Oh, great mountain,
you yield
unceasingly to the
softest,
formless,
everchanging...
river...

May I climb this cliff
of my life....
ever floating downstream....

Rapids

Glancing down
shimmering through
the rapids something
lay hidden.

In a moment
I knew
what I did not want
to know.

It was time,
time to dive in
over my head
deep into the river.

Ignoring the
part of me wanting
to stay dry
at all costs,
on the shore,
or in the boat...

Yet, there,
in the swift water
lay glimmering
my salvation,
and I knew it.

In leaping,
my faith grew...
like the small bird

who takes flight,
for the first time...

I felt the water
around me,
the rush
of being immersed...

Diving in deep,
over my head,
toward the radiance
calling me

My hands
reach out,
suddenly,
in contact with
earth, gravel,
smooth river rock,
and something else...

My eyes adjust,
the cool water,
clean and crystal clear,
and there...there,
a golden glow,
iridescent on the
riverbed.

Gold,
what a

thousand civilizations
have lived and died for,
lying here,
in my own life.

Light in the dark,
shining from below,
I cradled it,
and knew...

Within the rapids
of my life
lay hidden
treasure...

Sun Whispers

The sun
whispers to
my heart...
"Come out of your house,"
as the dawn
breaks open
a new day...

There is so much...
wanting to be seen,
heard, felt, and...
known...
I hurt...

And...yet...
I have no words to speak,
no poem to write,
no picture to paint.

Not here,
not now...
There is too much
muchness for that...

The dew-laden leaves,
the twisting branches
of some ageless inner fire,
the smell of soil

mingling with a thousand
birds singing
the sun up...

No...there is nothing,
nothing to do...
but go outside,
and obey the call...

Before it's too late...
and another sunrise
has melted away.

PORTALS

There are portals,
vortices like the one
that led to this birth...
And the one that
will lead through
death...

The only way in,
and the only way out
is through the bedrock
of experience...

As you leave,
there may be many
artifices erected in your mind...

Some good, some shaky,
but all borrowed unless
they resonate with the
knowing vibrations of
your own blood...

Seek then,
the meeting point
that lies within
and allows
true communion
with that greater
life...

Vibrating and pulsating
with the music
of eternity...

Success

You're a success today
if you are here
and present
to the murmurings
of this moment,
unimpeded by the
poisonous banterings
of a world gone mad.

You're a success today,
when you can look through
eyes, moist with compassion,
beholding the one you meet
with grace.

You are a success today,
in this moment, when you
 hear Grandmother Earth
call your name...
welcoming you to breathe
her air and walk upon her skin...

You are a success today
when you are one with
all things...
honoring the humble and simple
beings that come across your path...
...earthworm, grasshopper, and cricket...

You are a success today
when you no longer remain imprisoned

by the tar of regret,
but can stand naked in the wind,
and smile as you breathe in
the sweet fragrance of Now...

You are a success today
when you take my hand in yours
and look deeply in the eyes,
and honor the sanctuary that is
built by the word, "we"...

And you say it with the pain
and joy of knowing we are both united
and apart in a great dancing paradox...
that surrenders neither one of us,
as it dances us into the mystery of
communion...

Do not be shy,
do not deny today,
do not deny what you know...

Shout,
Shout out your truth!
before it's too late
and find the *success*
already living within you...

SOLSTICE

Waking out of my
slumber...
the mist rises
from my breath...
into the cool, crisp...
morning air...

Have I missed the sunrise?
This morning, the beginning of
the growth of a new year,
a new chapter, a new
beginning...

My tears fell last night
fully, deeply from a place,
seldom touched...
I feel a change stirring within
but, I can't see down the river...

I know the river is turning
in a direction I haven't been...
taking me toward a horizon
I can't yet see...

But...I see in front of me
this cool crisp morning
a horizon full of orange,
reds, and yellows...

No, I have not missed the sunrise...
glowing in the air...
hanging in the trees,
between the ocean and me...

Oh...how I drink this moment...

my tears flow through me now,
yet so differently from the longest
night of the year...

Today will be a few moments
longer than yesterday...
paving the way,
for growth, becoming,
and emergence...

Until I once again begin
the journey back towards
the darkness I only left
a few hours before...

How I love you, Life...
kaleidoscope of presence,
dancing feelings and a thousand
flames of insights, images and
flickering thought...

Blue to gold, gold to violet,
now streaks of white, oh,
could a sky be so...

Over the water now, as she
rises out of her slumber...
The rays of light
make a golden path
through the silent stillness
of the water...
beckoning...
inviting...
the day into being...

And...I am here, with my flute,
singing and playing to her...
and then there is no I...
no flute...no sunrise...there is...
this moment...
this communion...this...

Sunrise – December 23, 1999
(my daughter's 13th birthday) – following the winter solstice
night displaying the brightest full moon in 133 years

78

ONE DAY

One day, all this paper...
all this filing and saving the
precious shards of what we
"think" is important will fade.

One day,
people will live
from their hearts...
there will be Love...
and when there is love,
there is no need for
legislated rules...

But, we're young,
like the earth beginning
its grand march to waking.

Life begins to appear
small, barely perceptible,
movements, grotesque like
a jellyfish...

Billions of years
photosynthesis turns
these waring opposites,
wet and dry,
light and dark,
hard and soft,
fire and water,
spirit and matter...
into a dance
of being and becoming.

Now the Great Turning is upon us
and we like the plant people before us
are now given the task to
turn the suffering of life
into wisdom and compassion,
life into love...

We think we know what we need.
We think we know where we're going.
We think we know what we are doing
and what this is all about...

One day...
what we are here to give birth to
will make our toil, strained and oh,
so very confused strivings...like
coal, pressured into diamond...

One day...
our movements will be arabesque
dances radiating the diamond of love
that we are...

EARTH
MOMENTS

Never Ending

This conversation never ends...
and begins again with each you meet...

How, you ask?
By following the contours of the other's pain,
the geography of their suffering,
the geology of their love...

Follow these,
and they will lead you back
to the conversation with the belly of the earth
herself...

lying in wait...
for you...

Rings of Grace

Do you think the tree
knows how each branch will look?

Do you think the tree
plans its next gyration,
circling outward,
in God's rings of grace?

The tree
just allows the knowing to
branch, and twist,
and turn,
exactly where it is supposed to...

Trunk and roots
sigh deeply,
as those mysterious
unfoldings play and dance
until a new branch,
a new leaf,
a new seed
opens its sleepy eyes,
and says hello
to the world...

Out of a plan?
no...
out of love
life grows...

ETERNITY

Earth my home
for now...

I am star struck
while destined
to dust this planet
with the remnants of my body...

Yet, what is to become
of my soul?

I want to plumb the mystery that's me
I want to cry out
and yell and scream
for all eternity!

This word eternity, eternity
goes round and round
and round again...

I orbit this word
hoping it will point the way
to the territory
that it conjurs up
in my mind's eye...
short circuited from my heart
needing to reconnect
with my soul...

I sink these limbs of mine
into the earth
hoping they'll

take root
and grow ...

I fear
I've lost
the ability
to dig deep
into the dirt
and gather minerals
from the soil
to nourish my soul...

I want depth
to sink my teeth
and my limbs into.
To bury myself whole
within the earth
sending out rootlets
and finding a home
in this deep, dark, moistness...

Fearing neither darkness
nor the unknown,
rather,
taking hold, reaching deep
and sending out shoots into the unknown
I let my roots gather substance...
Reaching for the sun
and breaking through the soil
into the light....

It is then....
my soul propagates, splits and coagulates
into ever new and various forms...

For it's in the essence of this body,
where all there ever has been
and all there ever will be
breaks through
and reverberates
sending shock waves
through my spine...

Creator,
be the farmer
who tills the soil
of my soul
planting seeds
of secret eternity,
and the fruit I am
to bear...

MOONLIGHT

Moonlit night
and memories of
night crossings...

The full moon rises
like a lover who has
made short work of
my shyness...

I kiss her goodnight,
and she asks me to sleep
beneath her...steady, faithful,
unfailing...

Until she sets once more,
giving the night up to her
beloved sun...
dipping into oblivion...
once again...
out of love.

Moved, turned around
even upside down...
her breathless beauty
humbles me, and
I find myself...on my knees...
laughing, crying and grateful...

I see a halo around her now,
which begins to follow me,

and surround me
with a soft
incandescent glow...
and I realize...
I want no other moment...
no other life...
than this...
moonlit night...

River Banks

The movements of this moment
shift once again...

It isn't like a river,
it is a river...

This ever flowing on...

Through the rapids...
around the bends...
over the rocks,
and through the seemingly endless
valleys...

This water of life
like so many cross currents
of emotion,
struggles against the banks
ever on its way...

These banks,
define the river...

Even though it
battles against them...

It can't flow everywhere in all directions...
(although it wants to)
for if it did,
it would no longer be a river...

But this river that I am,
remembers, oh so vividly,
its life as ocean...

It is this memory that
carries me forward...
forever dreaming of uniting
once again...

In that endless embrace...
flowing in all directions...
the ocean of being...

Yet, in this in-between time...
betwixt the great waters defining
this river that I am...

I will know the struggle, and
toil of being only one thing.

A river flowing in this direction,
living this life that has been given
and no other...

This is the great paradox...

To be something, somebody,
in this life..

I must deny the very
essence that I am...

Everything...

Easy Prey

No,
I didn't choose...

No,
I didn't roam

No,
I didn't go in search
of this...

It found me
like easy prey.

Prey
caught on
the prairie
with
no place
to hide...

The talons
reached down,
and sank
into my back...

I cried out...
but,
there was
no one to
hear...

Not even
the groans
and moaning
of the earth
herself...

Just
the silent
quiet
unknowing,
of my own
pain.

Then...
in a moment
the pain
was gone

and
I...
I am flying,
above...

and down below
lies the
tattered,
torn body,
of my past life...

Today...
I am
Eagle...

and
the prison
guard
of my
old
world
has died...

and
I
have
much
work
to do...

Today...

ANCIENT FIRE

Like a glow
from some ancient fire,
out of the ruins
of the darkest night...

Although the cold
encased...
our heart's longing...

This dawn emerged...

Like a glow
from some ancient fire,
out of the ruins
of the darkest night...

Welcoming the journeyers
who danced on the lips
of insanity...
to the very end of the night...

The old woman whispered
to those who would listen
out of the trees,
and the windswept dunes...

"This night is every night...
and this dawn...
lasts forever..."

Like a glow
from some ancient fire,
out of the ruins
of the darkest night...

HUMAN

MOMENTS

BABBO'

Babbo,
do you remember the
evening on the back porch years ago?
Perhaps it was the blooming jasmine
that intoxicated us...

Perhaps it was the hibiscus
and gardenia...
or the twilight sky aglow
in hues of orange, red, and violet...

or that seductive sea breeze,
blowing steadily off the gulf as the sun set...

Whatever "it" was that prompted you
to share...I give thanks...

Do you remember what you said...
about us boys...your children?

I still hear your voice,
see the twinkle in your eye,
the glow of your skin...
when you spoke the words...

"When you were born...you boys...
were a miracle...you gave my life
more meaning than you will ever know..."
and then I felt the tears roll down your
face...

This tough man,
This hard man,
This man's man...

We held each other
until the mockingbird sang...
and the hummingbird collected nectar...
and the light dimmed...

Something in me was released that night...
when you spoke those words...
words I had never heard before...

Words that emerged with effort
and depth...
Words that touched those
parts of me seldom stirred...

Thank you Babbo...
for reminding me of
the miracle of a father's blessing...
the miracle of a man's tears...
the miracle of my love for you...
for you too...
my babbo,
my father...
are a miracle...

¹Babbo is the affectionate Italian word for father -
in the Tuscan dialect.

LAST MOMENTS

I enter the room...
and...
there you are...
sweet Elizabeth...
gift from God...
laying down...
for the last time...

Death has joined us here...
for our last meeting
body to body...

So simple, nothing fancy,
no casket, no elegant clothes,
your nightgown,
pale blue-green,
like the emerald sea...
smiling peacefully,
your hands folded
like a little girl
as you so often did...
reminding me of the little
girl...I always saw in your eyes...

Who believed in all things,
and loved all things...
and cared for all people...
no matter what they did,
no matter how they acted...

You taught me to pray
for all the world...
every night...

Even when you
dear and precious
Elizabeth
lived in hell...
you prayed...
for everyone...
and everything...

You knew,
where so many of us
just believe...
You knew Love,
a dancing with silence,
a making love to emptiness...
a talking to God...

And the angels talked back...

So here you are...
and here I stand...
speechless,
motionless,
except for the emergence of
something inside I can not hold back...

So many years of grief,
so many wounds unhealed...
I cry,
I sob,
for all the loss...
for all the missed moments...
for all the never-having-been...
I long,
for more time with you
my dear sweet Elizabeth...

One more hug,
one more kiss,
perhaps, just a whisper in my ear...

The memories flood me
cold walks by yourself,
a garden that you could never
share...

Fruit ripened on a vine
never picked.
Years of a visiting list,
left empty by other's fear...

Tears roll down,
and the quaking inside gives way to
sounds...

Is that me?
that horrendous grief?
that fearful blackness...
the unknown emptiness?
How much more can I take?
How much further must I fall?
Can I ever reach out again?
Can I ever love again?

Then as I held your hand
and touched your hair,
I heard the words
whispered in my ear...

"Michael, my dear sweet, precious
Michael...
Where are your tears taking you?

Do not fear, go deep, go far,
keep falling, until you are flying..."

One more deep guttural cry...
then I lose sense of
who I am, where I am,
when I am...

I am no more...
just pain,
hurt, and
grief...

No me, no
Elizabeth...
just the cry
of the Earth herself...

A cry echoing eternity,
shuddering even infinity...
breaking down every wall...

Then...

I feel an arm reach around me...
and I smell my dear
sweet Elizabeth and feel again
your embrace,
warm and near...
but not of flesh...
not of bone,
but of soul,
now complete...

And I hear a familiar hum,

a whisper, a "shhhh"...and I know
I have crossed over with you...
I take the feathers off
my flute...that I have carried,
at least a thousand miles
on foot...

I lay them over your heart,
and place the flowers there
too...and I know the feathers will
take you to God herself...
quickly and swiftly like
the eagle...

I tell the men I am ready,
as I wipe my tears,
and hold my flute saying,
"I must go with her"...

They wheel you out of the building and
across the street,
and we enter a room where they
said no one is to be...
I say, "I must, I have to be here!"
They relent...and let me go...
and I walk with you, and your
body's last moments on this earth...

I am glad I am with you,
and I hold your hand as they
open the oven door...

And I whisper softly to you,
and kiss your hair...
and you smile...

You are not afraid,
and now, no longer am I...
They slowly put you in,
the fire begins to roar,
and I take out my flute...
and I play like I have never
played before...

Oh, dear sweet Elizabeth...
I hear you going back home,
as the roar, and the heat,
and the music, create
all there is to know...

The tears flow again,
but different this time, they do not
take me down, but, this time
are lifting me up...

Then I feel you again...
and I close my eyes,
and we dance and dance,
as the fire roars...and
I feel joy in my heart,
and I celebrate your
new life...

Then, after a long while,
I go outside...and there...
rising above the fire is
heat dancing off the chimney
and the sun is shining.
A glorious day...and the
heat dances in shadows upon the tree...
and I know you are there waving at me...
through the dancing cherry tree...

and again, I play, and dance,
and sing...

and You, my dear sweet Elizabeth...
are here, today

Thank you for the gifts,
the smiles, the wounds and tears...

Thank you for never giving up,
or giving in and waiting for me
to grow and heal,
so now I can live,
love and be...

Without fear...

PILGRIM'S GLANCE

We are fragile creatures
born to be broken
and to die...

What is it
that brings us here
to suffer?

I do not know...
but one thing I do...
the walls standing between
you and me quietly fall
when we do not deny
this brokenness,
this vulnerability that
we are...

Join me then in this dance
of being and becoming,
and let the masks fall...
Now...before its too late,
and I miss the chance
to see you...
to really see into you...
and in so doing,
find myself...

Written for my soul friend and brother Hugh Carter
(Pilgrim) 1919-2007 a tireless pilgrim of love who practiced
letting the walls quietly fall every moment of his life.